#PATFACTS

DAILY INSPIRATION FROM ONE DREAMER TO ANOTHER

VOLUME 1

WRITTEN BY

Patrick Walker-Reese

PatrickWalkerReese

DESIGNED BY

Channing Bailey

ChanningBailey

ASPIRE™ BE THE DREAM.

ASPIREBETHEDREAM.COM

A Dream is something you belief in enough to work for. #PATFACTS are designed to ignite the dreamer in each one of us. In December 2013, I embarked on a journey that changed my life. I received my bachelors at Tennessee State University a few years early in 2010. After graduating from Tennessee State University, I spent three years working in some of the most underserved communities in the city. For three years, I poured everything I had into the lives of 30 middle school students and their families. By year four I began to ask myself, how do you sell hope to the hopeless? I learned the hard way that before you can help someone chase their dreams they must first have a dream. And more importantly, you must be actively chasing yours. In order to achieve your dreams you should be prepared for the sacrifices that dream chasing requires.

Success is a series of change, choices, and dreams

Do you believe in your dream enough to change your choices? Change is often the most difficult aspect of dreaming. At least it was for me. Your dreams will force you to change your environment, change your friends, and even change what you eat. I remember back to the beginning of my journey. I was in Atlanta with a group of high school seniors on a college tour staying at the Georgia Terrace Hotel across from the Fox Theatre. A light switched for me that trip. Maybe reading Robin Sharma's The Monk Who Sold His Ferrari or that I had gone without my routine turkey bacon for breakfast and survived inspired me. Whatever the case, I knew I needed discipline for this next stage of my life. Right then and there I put myself on a 40 day fast from all meat. These 40 days proved to be the launching point for a lasting lifestyle change. April 12th, 2013, the last day I ate meat. It is important to understand that change is inevitable. Being able to embrace this change is vital to success. Each day brings change. Those who adapt to it the quickest will be those who succeed. If you look at yourself and those around you a year from now and there has been no change, you have been doing something wrong. The first step towards achieving your dreams is to change the way you think. When you change your thoughts you change your world.

Once you've embraced and planned for change, you then realize the biggest change is your choices. Your dream will provide you with a lot more choices than you are used to, and fewer people capable of helping you make those choices. If you don't understand anything about choices understand this, the choices you make today will CHANGE YOUR LIFE. You will have to make some tough decisions enroute to your dreams. For instance, do I take the easy teacher and get an A or the hard teacher and learn? Do I go out or do I study? Do I spend money on this vacation or do I save and invest in myself? You will be faced with many choices only you can make. The true evidence of change is in those choices you've made. Your choices are a direct path to your dreams.

Your dreams should be valued as they are unique to you. They are snapshots of your desire. The things you dream about are the things you truly want in life. Wherever you are in your journey, today is the day to birth your dreams. Right now is the time to make your dream a reality. Whatever you dream of being tomorrow, you have to start being that today.

Almost five years ago I made the choice to live the life of my dreams. So can you.

This is vol. 1.

Patrick Walker-Reese
Dreamer

OFTEN TIME WE CLING TO THINGS THAT GIVE US IDENTITY OUT OF FEAR OF CREATING OUR OWN.

Don't be afraid to create the life you want. Your identity doesn't have to be connected to a job, a relationship, or an organization. If you're going to be defined by something, be defined by your passion. Let your dreams guide your life.

Potkinepo

Marszałkowska

501 519 520 521 525, N25 N31 N37 N75 N81

Poznańsk

Poznańska

ansoga

IT IS IMPOSSIBLE TO GET TO THE TOP WITHOUT LETTING GO OF THE THINGS THAT HELD YOU AT THE BOTTOM.

Change is inevitable. It is your choice if it's for better or for worse. Take the first step towards greatness and be okay with whatever is left behind. Sometimes all you can take with you to the top is you.

TO BE GREAT IS TO FALL IN LOVE WITH PRACTICE.

No matter what you do, you must love the art of getting better at it. You must become addicted to the process of becoming great. Get comfortable with being uncomfortable. Practice and repetition are the difference between good and great.

DON'T LET YOUR PURSUIT OF PERFECTION PROMOTE PROCRASTINATION.

So often we procrastinate waiting for things to be perfect. There will never be a perfect time, situation, or person. Pursue your passion, not perfection.

05

RARELY DO WE GET THE THINGS WE WAIT FOR, BUT WE ALMOST ALWAYS GET EXACTLY WHAT WE WORK FOR.

Good things come to those who work. Today is all you have, nothing after is promised. Do everything you can today to make tomorrow better. There is really no benefit in waiting. So don't wait for it, work for it.

MINUTES ARE LIKE DOLLARS, YOU CAN'T MAKE THE MOST OF THEM UNTIL YOU APPRECIATE THE VALUE OF EACH ONE.

You have to protect your most valuable asset. Time. Time is the one thing no one can give or buy. You can't win or earn more of it. When you begin to appreciate your time, you'll become more productive. Money will be the least of your worries, because even when you're in a tough place you must still focus on where your true value lies. Your time. Use it to chase your dreams.

YOU WILL NEVER BE GREAT UNTIL GOOD ISN'T GOOD ENOUGH.

If you're fine with being good then that's okay. But for those who want to be great, there is a simple solution - you must get sick and tired of good. Read what the greats read, and watch what the greats watch. Study the habits of greatness. You'll never be great as long as you're okay with good.

THERE ARE MANY THINGS YOU DON'T KNOW, THERE IS NOTHING YOU CAN'T LEARN.

As dreamers, we want to know it all. There's nothing wrong with not knowing, there's everything wrong with not wanting to know. Some people are born smart, but MOST people become smart. To begin the process of making a dream come true, you must learn everything you can about your craft. Read everything you can. Talk to everyone you can. The best dreamers are the best learners. In life there are always going to be things that you do not know, but there will be nothing you cannot learn.

PEOPLE RARELY REMEMBER WHAT YOU SAY, BUT THEY NEVER FORGET WHAT YOU DO.

Actions have, and always will, speak louder than words. People talk about their dreams all day, but a dream without action is dead. When you're gone people may not remember what you said but they'll always remember what you did, and how that made them feel. Start today by talking less and doing more. Put your ideas into action.

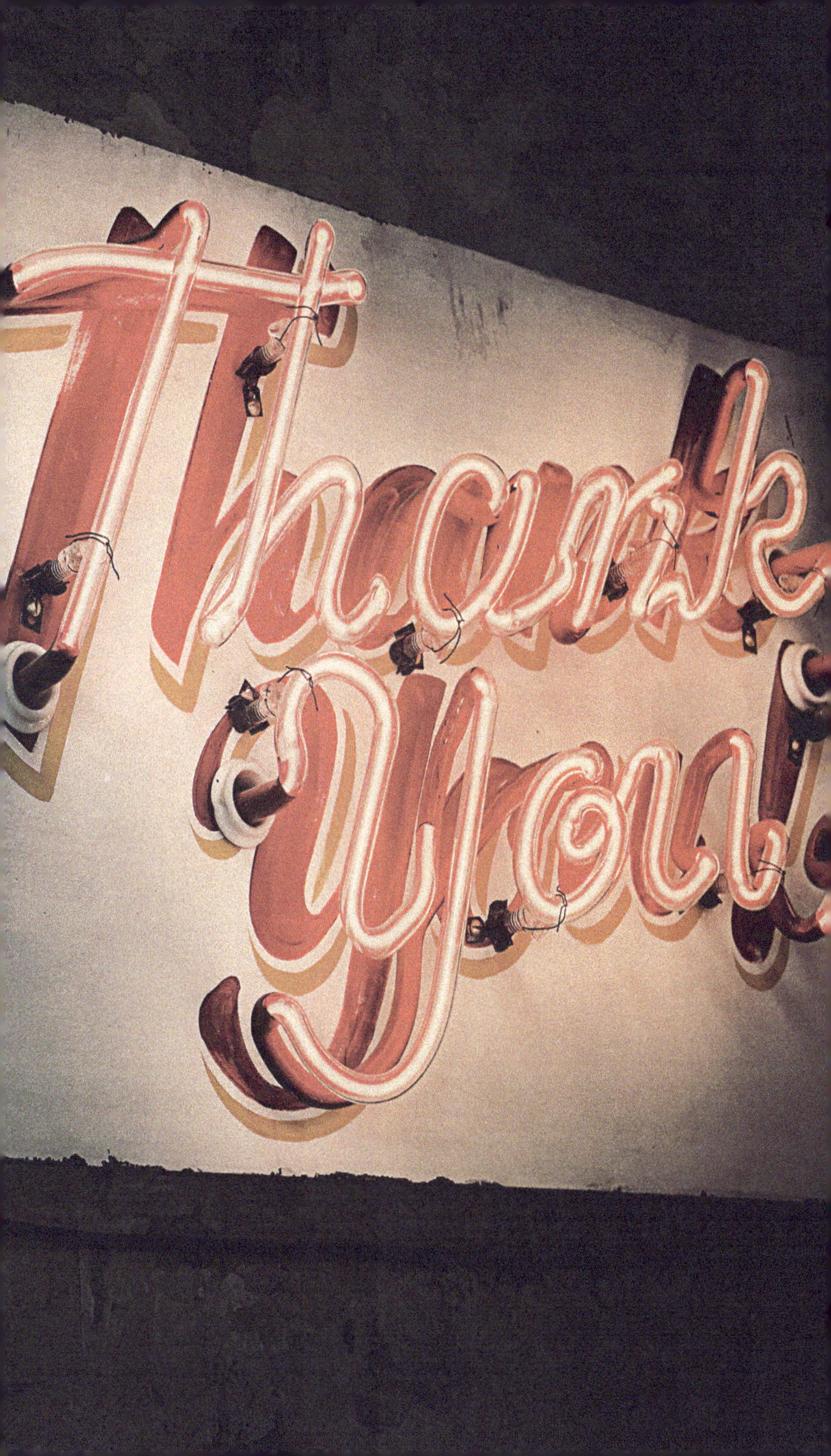

Thank You

MOST DREAMS BEGIN WITH UNPOPULAR DECISIONS.

Your dream won't make sense to everyone. More importantly, it doesn't have to. Don't be afraid to go against the grain, to step outside the box. Be confident to make the decisions that others wont. You can't get something that no one else has if you're doing what everyone else does.

BE CAREFUL WHAT YOU ACCEPT, IT MAY BECOME WHAT YOU EXPECT.

Never lower your expectations, no matter what or who is involved. Never accept less than your worth, no matter who's involved. Love yourself and your dreams enough to set high expectations and expect them to be met. The moment you begin to lower what you expect, you also lower what you accept. Your dream can't afford to accept anything less than the best.

IT'S NEVER TOO LATE TO START, BUT ITS ALWAYS TOO EARLY TO QUIT.

There is no timetable on your dream. Most dreams take years to accomplish. Everyday is a new opportunity to live the life you want. A new journey can begin at anytime, but quitting is forever. Don't be afraid to start even if you're not ready. But always be afraid to quit.

13

IN ORDER TO MOVE UP SOMETIMES YOU HAVE TO MOVE ON.

You can't take everything or everybody with you. Baggage can keep you down. In order to move forward you must first move past your present. Everybody wants to go to the top, but few people have the strength to leave the comfort of where they are. Moving up and moving on are synonymous, but moving on comes first.

YOU DON'T HAVE TO BE THE BEST IF YOU WORK HARDER THAN WHO'S BETTER.

The secret to success is simple. Work hard. There is no magic formula, and you don't have to be the best. You have to study the best. Study their process, and do more. There is always going to be someone smarter or more talented, but there is no excuse for someone working harder than you. You don't have to be the best but you have to work the hardest.

15

IF YOU DON'T LOVE IT, DO SOMETHING ELSE.

Love is the strongest emotion there is. Love hurts, love heals, love motivates. Life is too short for you to spend it doing something you don't love. It's not about loving your dream, though that's important. It's about loving yourself enough to dream. If you don't love it, leave it alone.

FAILURE AND SUCCESS ARE BOTH A CHOICE.

Success is the result of a series of choices. The beauty of life is that we get to choose who we want to be. We choose to be positive. We choose to be great. We also choose to fail or choose to succeed. As soon as you decide to succeed half the work is done. Life has many crossroads choose to be great at each one.

FINDING YOUR DREAM REQUIRES YOU TO QUESTION YOUR REALITY.

Question everything. Your dreams are not rooted in your reality. Dreams are the realities that we wish to create. It's not until we question how far we can go, that we begin to go as far as we can. Dreaming requires you to look past what you see, and believe in what you have not yet seen.

DREAM CHASERS RARELY SLEEP BECAUSE THEY ARE EXCITED ABOUT THE WORK THAT WAKING UP BRINGS.

A good dream makes it hard for you to sleep. Your dream should light a fire under you. Your dream should excite you and make you anxious. Your dream should become your alarm clock. Your dream should do more than wake you up. It should be the reason why you wake up.

19

EVERYONE FAILS, ONLY THE GREATS GET UP.

If you haven't failed you haven't tried hard enough. Failing is a part of dreaming. Everyone fails. It's not failing that makes you a failure, but quitting that makes you a failure. In life we are not defined by our failures, but by the times we get back up.

SUCCESS IS DOING WHAT YOU SAID YOU WOULD. EXCELLENCE IS DOING WHAT THEY SAID YOU COULDN'T.

Success is relative. Success is important but often overrated. Success is you accomplishing a predetermined goal. Excellence is you accomplishing your goals over and over again. Don't worry about people that say you can't. When you make it, they will be the first ones that said they knew you could.

JOBS GIVE YOU STABILITY, DREAMS GIVE YOU WINGS.

Every dream starts with a job. A job that shows us exactly what we don't want. Jobs give us security and safety. We feel good about jobs, we feel stable. Dreams give something that jobs can't. Dreams give you hope. Your dreams will take you to places that your job never will.

BE CAREFUL HOW YOU MEASURE SUCCESS, YOU MAY NEVER MEASURE UP.

Comparison is the easiest way to fail. Never measure your success by someone else's standards. Your dreams are unique, and they require unique sacrifices. Never measure yourself by other people's success, because their success will never measure up to your dreams.

DREAMS COME TRUE WHEN ALL NIGHTERS TURN INTO EVERY NIGHTERS.

Dreams do come true. You can accomplish things you never thought you could, if you work like you never thought you could. Turn staying up all night into staying up every night, until you're living the life you used to dream about at night.

SUCCESS DOES NOT COME FROM PERFECTION, BUT FROM PERSISTENCE.

Perfection cannot be accomplished but it can be pursued. Practice having patience. Understand that this is a long journey. Sometimes it's not about who can work the hardest, but who can work the hardest, the longest.

IF YOU'RE COMPETING WITH ME AND I'M COMPETING WITH MYSELF, I WILL ALWAYS BE ONE STEP AHEAD.

Push yourself. Sometimes success is about taking one more step, doing one more rep, being a little more patient. You can't run any race but your own. Prepare for success by staying one step ahead of yourself.

#PATFACTS IS A COLLECTION OF THOUGHTS, REFLECTIONS, AND MANTRAS THAT HELPED PATRICK WALKER-REESE (PWR) ALONG HIS JOURNEY.

#Patfacts are daily inspirations from one dreamer to another. In December of 2012, PWR quit his salaried position with a respected and award winning non- profit and a month later founded Aspire, in January of 2013.

Aspire is a motivational consulting firm that specializes in highly interactive motivational presentations and workshops. Now in its forth year of operation Aspire has worked with varied reputable organizations and companies such as, Caterpillar Financial, Metro Nashville Public Schools, New York City Department of Youth and Community Development, YMCA, Fisk University, Tennessee State University, and a host of professional athletes.

His journey from troubled youth to Dream Builder has been one of both trial and triumph. In his debut book, PWR opens up about the highs and lows of dream chasing through a series of quotes, or #Patfacts, aimed to inspire dreamers from all walks of life. He seeks to motivate the reader to dream bigger and work harder than ever before, because dreams come true everyday.

THE ONLY THING MORE POWERFUL THAN A DREAM
IS THE ACTION YOU PUT BEHIND IT.

PATRICKWALKERREESE.COM

PWR

www.ingramcontent.com/pod-product-compliance
Lightning Source LLC
Chambersburg PA
CBHW040744160426
R18147200001B/R181472PG42813CBX00002B/3

9 780989 696159